*The
Connell Short Guide
to*

President Truman
and Post-War America
1945–1953

*by
Patrick Andelic*

Contents

Introduction	3
A failed haberdasher: from Independence to the White House, 1884-1945	4
The Cold War, 1945-1948	13
Why did Truman drop the atomic bomb?	24
The whistlestop campaign, 1948	28
The Fair Deal	32
Korea and McCarthy, 1949-1953	36
Harry Truman and the historians	44

NOTES

Five facts about Harry S. Truman	*25*
Chronology	*48*
Bibliography	*50*

Introduction

Harry S. Truman was one of the unlikeliest American presidents in the 20th century. Indeed, until a few months before he assumed the office in April 1945, charged with resolving wars in Europe and Asia and then managing the transition to a "Cold War" with the Soviet Union, he may never have seriously thought about the White House at all. Modest and unassuming, Truman had failed in business before entering politics, and was widely thought to be a competent but undistinguished senator. He was an accidental president, taking the office on the death of his more popular predecessor. He would leave that office with the lowest approval ratings of any president in the modern era. Yet today many judge him one of the most important American leaders.

Stephen Graubard dubbed Truman "The Creator" in his collection of presidential biographies.* He oversaw the US's rise to superpower status, the huge social and economic changes that followed World War II, the opening skirmishes of the Cold War with the Soviet Union, and the transformation of the Democratic Party. The decisions he made in approaching these challenges were felt long after he left office. Without his administration, post-war America would have

* Stephen Graubard, *The Presidents: The Transformation of the American Presidency from Theodore Roosevelt to Barack Obama*, p.299

looked utterly different.

Robert Dallek ranks Truman as one of the four great presidents of the 20th century, alongside Theodore Roosevelt, Woodrow Wilson, and Franklin D. Roosevelt. But he distinguishes Truman from the others "for his ordinariness". "How he rose above the commonplace to become so extraordinary makes Truman's life and career a compelling puzzle": this is the conundrum at the centre of this short guide.*

A failed haberdasher: from Independence to the White House, 1884-1945

Truman's beginnings were humble. He was born on 8 May 1884, to a family of Scots-Irish farmers in southern Missouri. His early childhood memories were happy, though the family's finances were often shaky. When Truman was six years old his family moved to Independence, Missouri, which was, in David McCullough's words, "a sleepy backwater, churchgoing, conservative, rooted to the past, exactly as most residents preferred".**

Truman recalled later that he had not been popular as a boy. "The popular boys were the ones

* Robert Dallek, *Harry S. Truman* (2008), p.1.
** David McCullough, *Truman* (1992), 50.

who were good at games and had big, tight fists ... [T]o tell the truth, I was kind of a sissy."* The young Truman was very short-sighted ("blind as a mole," he said) and this made him bookish and withdrawn. His mother bought him an expensive pair of spectacles from Kansas City, which made him something of a curiosity in his home town. He spent long hours in the Independence town library, reading reams of history books. (History provided, he said later, "solid instruction and wise teaching".) He also loved the novels of Mark Twain and Sir Walter Scott.

Truman was one of the few boys in Independence to attend high school (girls outnumbered boys three-to-one in his class). A gifted student, he skipped the third grade and went directly into the fourth. He was a talented and enthusiastic piano player, which also marked him out from the other boys in Independence – and young Harry endured some ridicule for it.

In the fourth grade, Truman met Elizabeth "Bess" Wallace. Bess's family lived two blocks away from the Trumans, and she sat behind Harry in most of his classes. She was popular and athletic – she played baseball and tennis, ice skated, and danced – and Truman was smitten. "If I succeeded in carrying her books to school for her and back home for her I had a big day."** Towards the end of

---

* Alonzo L. Hamby, *Man of the People: A Life of Harry S. Truman* (1995), p.3.
** McCullough, 49.

1910 (when he was 26), Truman began courting Wallace, the only serious romantic interest of his life.

Harry's father, John Truman, bankrupted himself through poor investments and the Truman family lost their farm in 1901, when Harry was 17. Truman's poor eyesight put an end to his dream of a place at America's most prestigious military academy, West Point. Instead, he did jobs in the mailroom of the Kansas City Star, as a railroad timekeeper, and as a bank clerk. He joined the National Guard in 1905, sporadically participating in its activities until 1911, when he let his commission lapse.

In 1906, at his father's insistence, Truman returned to manage the farm that his family had reacquired. He disliked farming and, after his father's death in 1914, began to look for new opportunities. His search proved fruitless for several years and he lost a lot of money on mining and oil-exploring ventures. He remained a farmer until 1917 when, after the US entered the First World War, he re-enlisted in his National Guard artillery unit. At 33, Truman was older than most recruits, and past draft age. But he had been inspired, he wrote later, by President Woodrow Wilson's idealistic rhetoric about the US coming to the aid of European democracy. "I felt like Galahad after the Grail," Truman wrote in his autobiography.*

---

* Dallek, 3.

In July 1918, Captain Truman was dispatched to France in command of the regiment's Battery D. When he took command, the unit had a reputation for being ill-disciplined. He distinguished himself as their commanding officer, however, winning praise and popularity among his men for his firm leadership style. Battery D saw action as part of the Meuse-Argonne offensive in late 1918, providing support to infantry battalions, though Truman's unit did not lose a single man.

In 1919, he returned to Independence and married Bess. Their daughter, Mary Margaret, was born in 1924. She grew up to become a singer and author of crime novels and biographies, including a presidential biography of her father.

Truman started a haberdashery (a men's clothing store specialising in small items for sewing such as buttons and ribbons) in downtown Kansas City with an army buddy, Edward Jacobson. The store prospered for a few years but was forced to close in 1922 in the midst of a severe post-war recession. Truman refused to file for bankruptcy and it was a decade before he was able fully to clear the debts that he accumulated from this business.

After the failure of his business ventures, politics was Truman's salvation. As he joked when asked why he had gone into politics, "I have to eat".* His family supported the Democratic Party and had been involved to varying degrees in state Democratic

---

* Aida D. Donald, *Citizen Soldier: A Life of Harry S. Truman* (2012), 74.

politics since 1900, when his father took him to his first Democratic National Convention, held in Kansas City. After the war, he became more involved with the Kansas City machine, then under the control of a boss called Tom Pendergast. Political machines were once a key feature of American politics, particularly in cities. Essentially, a machine was a political organisation headed by a powerful "boss" (or sometimes group of bosses) whose power stemmed from their ability to dole out patronage, usually jobs for supporters and contracts for local businesses.

In 1922, with the backing of the Pendergast machine – he was introduced by his friend, Jim Pendergast, the boss's nephew – Truman was elected County Court judge of Jackson County's eastern district. Initially, it seemed that Truman's political career would be as rocky and short-lived as his business career – he lost his bid for re-election in 1924. However, Truman's support from Pendergast meant that he soon returned to office. In 1926, when he ran for the post of presiding judge of Jackson County, he was elected unopposed. When he ran for re-election in 1930, his majority more than tripled. Though, while in office, he ignored the criminal activities of his patrons in the machine – corruption, graft, and election-rigging – Truman was generally respected as honest. He was proud of the fact that he never used his office to personally enrich himself. "I will be a pauper when

President Truman signing a proclamation initiating America's involvement in the Korean War

I'm done," he said.*

Truman's time as presiding judge coincided with the beginning of the Great Depression, the deepest and longest economic recession in US history, which began in 1929 and would continue until the Second World War. As a heavily agricultural state, Missouri was particularly badly hit, and the plight of the state's farmers would be a huge influence on Truman's politics in the 1930s. After Democrat Franklin D. Roosevelt (FDR) became president in 1933 promising a "New Deal" for the American people, Truman was appointed director of the Federal Re-Employment Program, part of the

* Donald, 90.

newly-created Civil Works Administration (CWA), putting Missourians into jobs. The appointment came from Pendergast, who had been FDR's key backer in the state, and the experience turned Truman into an enthusiastic supporter of Roosevelt's New Deal.

By now a fixture of Missouri politics, Truman began contemplating a bid for a state-wide office, either governor or senator. Initially, Pendergast was not supportive of Truman's ambitions, but he reluctantly supported Truman as Senate candidate in 1934, after being rejected by his favoured candidates. With the backing of the Kansas City machine, Truman won the primary and the general election. In the Senate, Truman was disdained by some liberals for his links with machine politics. The *New York Times* dismissed him as "a rube [yokel] from Pendergast land" while managing to get his first name wrong ("Henry").* He was, however, generally popular in the Senate, well-liked for his work ethic and genial demeanour.

Truman's time in Congress coincided with the burst of reform legislation that historians have called the "Second New Deal", most notably the Social Security Act, which created a national pension system, and the Wagner Act, which guaranteed Americans' right to join a trade union, both passed in 1935 – with Truman's vote. Truman was largely loyal to Roosevelt, with a few exceptions.

---

* Dallek, 10.

(He refused, for instance, to support FDR's chosen candidate for Senate Majority Leader, Alben Barkley of Kentucky.)

In 1939, Tom Pendergast was imprisoned for tax evasion. Truman had stoutly defended his patron throughout the trial, which damaged his reputation. When he ran for re-election in 1940, most of Missouri's major newspapers opposed him and the Roosevelt administration offered no help, but Truman was still re-elected. A key bloc in his winning coalition was Missouri's African-American voters; Truman was ahead of much of his party on the question of civil rights and had supported anti-lynching legislation in the Senate.

The Second World War dominated Truman's second Senate term, as the US began to offer increasing support to the Allies in the war in Europe. Truman was supportive of FDR's efforts to edge the US closer to the action, voting for Lend-Lease, the programme that enabled the Allies to buy US weapons and supplies on credit. Early in 1941, Truman proposed a special select committee to investigate fraud and waste among defence contractors who received contracts from the federal government to meet the nation's increasing military expenditures. The result was the Senate Special Committee to Investigate the National Defense Program. Though initially small and poorly-funded, what became known as the "Truman Committee" turned the Missouri senator into a national figure. Truman's committee toured the country, held hundreds of hearings, called thousands of witnesses, issued 51 reports, and saved the US government a reported $15 billion.* In March 1943, "Investigator Truman" was featured on the cover of *Time* magazine.

Truman's work as part of the select committee marked him out as a possible running mate for Roosevelt, as the president prepared to seek his fourth term in office in 1944. Democratic Party leaders had been growing increasingly worried about Roosevelt's vice president, Henry Wallace, who they thought was too left-wing. By this time Roosevelt's health was failing and there was a real concern that the president might not survive a fourth term. Therefore, whoever was chosen as vice president was likely to end up as president. Though Truman was a plausible option, popular with conservatives and liberals in the party, he was still not the obvious choice.

Thanks to the machinations of party leaders and the president himself, Truman was nominated at the convention, and the Roosevelt-Truman ticket went on to win the general election by a large margin. But Vice President Truman was not a confidante of Roosevelt's. There was no effort to prepare him for the responsibilities that would fall upon his shoulders if FDR were to die. Truman recalled that, in the nearly three months he served as FDR's vice-president, "I don't think I saw him

---

* Donald, 116.

but twice... except at Cabinet meetings". However, on 12 April 1945, only 82 days after he had become vice president, Truman was summoned to the White House and told that Franklin Roosevelt had succumbed to a fatal cerebral haemorrhage at his Georgia retreat. Harry S. Truman was now president.

The Cold War, 1945-1948

"Boys, if you ever pray, pray for me now," Truman told reporters after he was sworn in as the 33rd president. "When they told me yesterday what had happened [Roosevelt's death] I felt like the moon, the stars, and all the planets had fallen on me." The challenges facing Truman were certainly daunting. He was taking command of a nation that was in effect still fighting two wars, against the Japanese Empire in the Pacific and against the Axis powers in Europe. The war against Nazi Germany and its allies was drawing to a close (and indeed the Third Reich would formally surrender within a month of Truman taking office), but the war against Japan seemed likely to drag on. Assuming both conflicts could be concluded swiftly, Truman was still faced with the problems of managing the U.S.'s return to peacetime and also of overseeing the birth of the post-war world.

Throughout his presidency, Truman suffered from comparisons with his predecessor. He lacked

Roosevelt's aristocratic grace and confidence and his easy charm. Roosevelt, noted one journalist, "looked imperial, and he acted that way, and he talked that way. Harry Truman... looked and acted and talked like – well, a failed haberdasher".

Truman sought to build public confidence in his presidency by carrying on Roosevelt's agenda. His first official act was publicly to announce that the organising conference of the United Nations (UN) would go ahead in San Francisco on April 25. FDR had been strongly identified with the creation of a world organisation to promote international co-operation and settle disputes between nations, and had in fact coined the term "United Nations" to describe it. Truman underscored his commitment to the organisation by appointing FDR's widow, Eleanor Roosevelt, as a US delegate to the UN General Assembly in December 1945.

Truman's immediate priority on assuming office, however, was ending the Second World War. He committed himself to FDR's objective of unconditional surrender from both Germany and Japan. The Nazi regime surrendered within days, but the war in the Pacific carried on until August. Truman's initial hopes of forcing a speedy Japanese capitulation rested on convincing the Soviets to launch an invasion of Japan after the end of the war in Europe. At the Potsdam Conference in July 1945 – his first international conference as one of the Big Three (the leaders of the US, UK, and Soviet Union) – Truman received a reaffirmation of an earlier promise from Joseph Stalin that a Soviet invasion of Japan would begin in August, a commitment that was written into the conference declaration.

The situation changed dramatically when Truman learned that scientists working for the Manhattan Project (a research project led by the US, with the support of the UK and Canada) had successfully tested an atomic bomb. Truman received the news of the first successful test while at Potsdam. On August 6, on Truman's orders, the first atomic bomb ever used in war was dropped on Hiroshima. Two days later, on August 8, a second bomb was dropped on Nagasaki. Japan surrendered on August 11. The precise reasons behind Truman's decision to drop the bomb have been the subject of enormous controversy ever since, as discussed in more detail later.

Behind the decisions taken by the US as the war came to an end was the question of relations with the Soviet Union, and how those relations would define the post-war order. The Second World War had left the United States and the Soviet Union as the only two superpowers. Initial hopes that wartime alliance could endure into peacetime soon vanished and were replaced by a rivalry that came to be called the "Cold War".

Some historians, such as Frank Costigliola, have suggested that Truman's abrasive personality was a key cause of the Cold War. Roosevelt, they suggest, would have been able to handle the Soviets with more skill and tact.* Certainly, Truman was a less adept diplomat than the more experienced and cosmopolitan Roosevelt had been during the war. However, realising his shortcomings, he went to great lengths to prepare himself, staying up long into the night reading State Department briefing papers.

The status of Eastern Europe was the most important issue in the negotiations between the US and the Soviet Union as the war drew to a close. The war ended with the USSR occupying all of Eastern Europe and Stalin, who wanted security for the Soviet Union and his own regime, did not intend to relax his hold on those nations. The Truman administration pressed the Soviet regime to honour its promises to hold free elections in Eastern European states – whether out of genuine commitment to democracy or a more self-interested desire to lessen Soviet power still divides historians. On April 23, 1945, Truman had a famous meeting with Soviet Foreign Minister Vyacheslav Molotov, during which he berated Molotov for the Soviet failure to hold elections in Poland. Truman claimed later that when a shaken Molotov had declared, "I have never been talked to like that in my life", he had replied: "Carry out your agreements and you won't get talked to like that."

Truman also faced the problems of managing America's transition to peace. The war had finally

* Frank Costigliola, *Roosevelt's Lost Alliances: How Personal Politics Helped Start the Cold War* (2013).

ended the Depression – the chronically high unemployment rate of the 1930s vanished as the US mobilised to defeat fascism. From Truman down, there were fears that the US would slump back into economic recession after the war, as it did after World War One. Truman called on Congress to pass a range of laws building on the New Deal: for full employment and anti-discrimination in hiring, housing, aid for farmers and small businesses, national health insurance and an expanded social security system. Conservative Southern Democrats had become more dominant in the Congress since the New Deal's heyday, however, and Truman's agenda largely stalled.

Nonetheless, peace did not produce recession. The demobilisation of the enormous US armed forces (12 million at their peak) was aided by the Servicemen's Readjustment Act, or the "G.I. Bill of Rights", which provided funds for education and job retraining for veterans. There was also a consumer boom after years of wartime rationing. But the transition was not entirely smooth. Truman had to deal with labour unrest and a wave of strikes between 1945-1946. In one instance, the president used his wartime powers to temporarily nationalise the coalmines.

The problem of how to handle the Soviet Union remained the principal one confronting the Truman administration. The shaky wartime alliance was starting to break down and the relationship between the US and Soviet Union was becoming increasingly antagonistic. In March 1946, the former British prime minister, Winston Churchill, gave a speech at Westminster College, Missouri, in which he declared that "an iron curtain" had descended across the European continent and called for "a special relationship" between the US and UK to resist Soviet expansionism. Truman had arranged the invitation for Churchill, travelled to Fulton with him by train, and sat behind him as he delivered his famous words.* Stalin interpreted this speech as "a call to war with the Soviet Union".

A month before Churchill delivered the "Iron Curtain" speech, a young diplomat in the US embassy in Moscow, George Kennan, sent a communication back to Washington outlining the ideology that would define Truman's Soviet policy. Kennan was an expert on Russia and deputy head of the Moscow embassy. His 8,000-word cable of February 1946, known as the "Long Telegram", made a huge splash when it landed in Washington. Kennan wrote that concessions would make the Soviet Union bolder; it would only behave more reasonably if it encountered a string of failures. What was needed was "long-term, patient but firm and vigilant *containment* of Russian expansive tendencies".

That word of Kennan's – "containment" – would become central to US policy towards the Soviet Union for at least a generation. Rather than directly

---

* Churchill was the first to use this term, "special relationship", about the UK-US alliance.

President Truman and Prime Minister Winston Churchill leave the "Little White House," the residence of President Truman during the Potsdam Conference.

confront the Soviet Union, and risk war, the US would choose key moments to resist Soviet ambitions. Though it was classified, the Long Telegram was widely circulated in Washington.

In the early years of the Cold War, Europe became the testing ground for "containment". The Truman administration had been increasingly concerned that post-war discontent in Europe might lead to Communist takeovers. Greece emerged as a particular trouble spot. Britain had been giving military support to Greece's Royalist government in its civil war with Communist insurgents but, as a result of the weakening UK economy, that commitment could no longer be sustained. The US worried that Britain's withdrawal would create a vacuum that the Soviets would rush to fill.

Under-secretary of State Dean Acheson, a staunch anti-Communist, told Truman that if Greece went Communist, Turkey would as well, and then the whole region might follow. One rotten apple, said Acheson, would spoil the whole barrel. Persuaded that the US needed to take action, Truman, on March 12, 1947, in an address to Congress, declared that it "must be the policy of the United States to support free peoples who are resisting attempted subjugation by armed minorities or by outside pressures". The principles the president outlined in this speech, which collectively became known as the "Truman Doctrine", would define American policy for an entire generation. Wherever free nations were threatened by domestic insurgencies, invasion, or diplomatic pressure, the US would provide political, economic, and/or military aid. Days after Truman's speech, Congress voted to appropriate $400 million for Greece and Turkey.

The Truman Doctrine was only the start of America's involvement in post-war Europe. Within months, the US would embark on a far more expansive plan to rebuild the shattered European nations: the Marshall Plan. In early 1947, newly-appointed Secretary of State George Marshall set off on a tour or Europe and was shocked by the devastation he encountered. He was particularly outraged by what he saw as America's dithering over aid. "The patient is sinking while the doctors deliberate," he said. The Truman Doctrine had created the precedent for interventions by the US. The next plan was to be Europe-wide, covering even nations within the Soviet sphere of influence – and the Soviets themselves.

With Truman's backing, Marshall announced his plan in a speech at Harvard University on June 5, 1947. If the US did not help Europe in its hour of need, he argued, "economic, social, and political deterioration of a very grave character would follow". The US, said Marshall, "should provide a cure rather than a mere palliative". Following this speech, with Truman's backing, Marshall invited the European nations to devise a rescue package. A conference was convened in Paris, with the participation of 16 nations, including the Soviet Union. The Soviet representatives eventually walked out of the conference, objecting to the very idea of a "Europe-wide" plan and suggesting that each nation prepare their own individual plan. A week after walking out, the Kremlin announced its own scheme, the "Molotov Plan", for the Eastern European states. Poland and Czechoslovakia withdrew from the talks shortly afterwards for fear of angering the Soviets.

The Paris conference ultimately produced a plan that called for $28 billion in economic aid for Western Europe over a four-year period. The Truman administration accepted the plan in broad terms, but reduced the dollar amount to $19 billion before sending it to Congress in December 1947. The plan ran aground in a hostile Congress, which was now dominated by Republicans after the midterm elections of 1946. With Truman increasingly unpopular, and Americans anxious to cut back spending after the war, it seemed that the plan was doomed. But a Communist coup in Czechoslovakia in February 1948 spurred Congress to authorise the Marshall Plan. It would, in the end, total $17 billion, and Marshall himself would receive the Nobel Peace Prize in 1953. Truman described his Doctrine and the Marshall Plan as "two halves of the same walnut", two elements of the same containment policy.

Fearing what they saw as a hostile Western conspiracy, the Soviets struck back in Berlin. After the war, Germany was divided into four zones controlled by the Allied powers (Britain, the US, France, and the USSR). Berlin, within the Soviet zone, had been likewise divided into four sectors. By 1948, the three non-Soviet powers had reached a series of agreements to unify their zones into "West Germany". The Soviets reasoned that this indicated that the other powers had abandoned their original hopes of reunifying Germany's Western and Eastern sections, and thus there was no reason for Berlin, which would now be permanently in the Soviet zone, to remain divided and partly under the control of the Western powers. In June 1948, the Soviets announced a blockade of all road, rail, and water traffic entering West Berlin. The only routes into the city that remained open were three narrow air corridors that allowed planes to enter. There was no way to stop a supply plane without shooting it down, which would have been an act of war. West Berlin was left in a state of siege and on the brink of starvation.

Although some in Washington were sympathetic to the idea of abandoning West Berlin to the Soviets, Truman was not among them. "We are going to stay, period," he said. He ordered an unprecedentedly huge airlift, resupplying Berlin from the air. At one point, a plane was landing every minute. The Soviets lifted the blockade in May 1949, having failed to force West Berlin to capitulate, and the same month a German Democratic Republic (GDR) was established in East Germany, formalising the split into two German states. This was a symbol of the hostility that had crystallised between the US and USSR. The Cold War was under way.

Why did Truman drop the atomic bomb?

Truman was only informed of the existence of the atomic bomb at the end of his first cabinet meeting as president, when Secretary of War Henry Stimson took him aside and told him that the US had a weapon of "almost unbelievable destructive power", a weapon so secret that not even the Congress had been informed. Truman's decision to use this weapon against Japan a few months later has been the subject of intense controversy, not only moral controversy (can it ever be justified to use a weapon with such an indiscriminately destructive impact?) but also controversy among historians: why did Truman decide to use the A-bomb?

The orthodox interpretation, advanced by historians such as Herbert Feis and Robert Newman, holds that the president's decision was essentially military: that the intention was to shorten the war and spare American lives. These historians accept Truman's own justification for using the bomb and that of other officials in his administration. With the publication of Gar Alperovitz's *Atomic Diplomacy: Hiroshima and Potsdam* in 1965, however, a new revisionist interpretation began to rise. This interpretation is based on the argument that the use of nuclear weapons was militarily unnecessary and that the real reason for dropping

FIVE FACTS ABOUT HARRY S. TRUMAN

1. Truman had the shortest middle name of any U.S. president. In fact, he only had a middle initial: "S". This was chosen to please his grandfathers, Anderson Shipp Truman and Solomon Young.

2. As a young man, Truman took pride in the fact that he had read every book in the Independence Public Library.

3. As president, Truman kept a sign on his desk that announced, "The Buck Stops Here". Truman's sign was an acknowledgement that he was prepared to make tough decisions as president.

4. Truman survived an assassination attempt in 1950 when two Puerto Rican nationalists attempted to shoot him in Blair House (the Trumans were staying there while the White House underwent renovations). They never made it to Truman, but a guard was killed.

5. Truman is the only U.S. president since 1901 not to have held a college degree.

the bomb was to intimidate the Soviet Union with its awesome capabilities and make them easier to handle in post-war negotiations.

Orthodox historians point to the fact that American planners had concluded that an invasion of Japan could result in 250,000 Allied casualties and many more Japanese losses. There was also a high risk that 100,000 Allied prisoners-of-war might be executed when the invasion began. These figures were supported by the heavy losses that the US had sustained as it advanced towards Japan across the Pacific. The Battle of Iwo Jima, for instance, which began in February 1945 and lasted for six weeks, resulted in 7,000 US dead and 20,000 casualties. Clearly, ran the orthodox view, the administration concluded it would be irresponsible not to use a weapon that had the potential to save so many American lives.

Revisionists counter that not only was Japan on the verge of collapse by summer 1945, but that Truman and other policymakers understood this. Prior to the first successful test of the bomb, the US had been anxious for the Soviets to join the war against Japan but, argue the revisionists, once it was clear the bomb worked, the Truman administration became determined to ensure that the Japanese surrendered quickly, preventing the Soviets from gaining territories in Asia, as they had in Eastern Europe. Indeed, the Soviets did begin attacking the Japanese possession of Manchuria on 8 August, between the dropping of the bombs on

Hiroshima and Nagasaki. Revisionists also point to the fact that Stalin interpreted the nuclear weapon as an American ploy. "A-bomb blackmail is American policy," he said.*

There is no decisive piece of evidence on either side. Most historians now agree that there was a mix of motives behind Truman's decision but that his desire to end the war quickly was both genuine and the most important consideration. Nonetheless, American policymakers recognised that the bomb would be a crucial bargaining chip in post-war negotiations with the Soviets, and that a successful demonstration of its power would strengthen their hand.

There are other factors that should be taken into account as well – for instance, the desensitising effect that US aerial bombing of Japan had on assessments of whether the A-bomb was a significant step up. The air raid on Tokyo in March 1945, which had lasted for two hours, had destroyed 16.5 square miles of the city and killed 100,000 civilians. After years of such brutality, it was easier to accept that the A-bomb was a legitimate weapon. Racism, too, was a factor. Truman confided in his diary that he expected the Japanese to fight like "savages, ruthless, merciless, and fanatic". That he perceived the Japanese in such terms undoubtedly made it easier to drop the bomb. Whatever the precise mix of reasons, Truman never wavered in

---

* John Lewis Gaddis, *The Cold War* (2005), 26.

his public rationale: that the dropping of the atomic bombs was necessary to foreshorten the war and save American lives. "I regarded the bomb as a military weapon," he said later, "and never had any doubt that it should be used."

The whistlestop campaign, 1948

The start of Truman's term had been rocky. He had suffered in comparisons with FDR and had failed his first electoral test, the congressional elections of 1946, when the Republicans had won both houses of Congress for the first time since 1932. From a peak of 87 per cent approval in Gallup polling in June 1945, Truman's approval rating had tumbled to 52 per cent by June 1946. His domestic agenda stalled during his first term. Indeed, the only significant piece of legislation that emerged was the Taft-Hartley Act, passed by the Republican Congress over Truman's veto, which limited the ability of labour unions to organise.

No longer facing the wily Roosevelt, Republicans were confident that they could defeat his apparently slow-footed successor in the 1948 presidential election. Truman was often disparaging about the presidency (he famously called the White House "the great white jail"), but he had a strong desire to win an election in his own right. His approval ratings began to climb in 1947, but he was still considered an underdog for re-election by many observers. Indeed, it was by no means a sure thing that he could even win his party's nomination. Many liberals hoped to dump Truman as a candidate in favour of Henry Wallace, the former vice president and Secretary of Agriculture.

Truman needed something daring to give his campaign a much-needed boost. Often clumsy and uninspiring when giving formal speeches, he was much better as an extemporaneous speaker. His staff took advantage of this with a campaign tour that ensured Truman's re-election efforts would pass into campaign lore. The president embarked on a two-week 30,000-mile cross-country tour by train. The last car of the train, in which the president rode, was outfitted with a large rear platform, a lectern, and loudspeakers. The train would stop at numerous stations – or "whistle-stops" – where crowds would gather to listen to the pugnacious Truman denounce Congress and discuss the challenges ahead. These appearances were informal and unstructured – at one stop in California, the leader of the free world appeared on the platform in his dressing gown and pyjamas – but they proved to be remarkably effective.

At the party's national convention in Philadelphia in July 1948, Truman was nominated on the first ballot. The most dramatic confrontation at that convention came over the issue of civil rights for African-Americans. A group of liberals led by

Minneapolis mayor Hubert Humphrey, who was then bidding for one of Minnesota's Senate seats, successfully persuaded the convention to vote for their more robust civil rights plank as part of the national platform. The climax came when Humphrey took to the stage and implored his party "to get out of the shadow of states' rights and to walk forthrightly into the bright sunshine of human rights".* The speech prompted a walkout by Southern Democrats, who went on to form their own States' Rights or "Dixiecrat" Party, nominating South Carolina governor Strom Thurmond as their presidential candidate.

Truman delivered a pugnacious acceptance speech, telling the cheering delegates that he was going to "win this election and make these Republicans like it – don't you forget that!". He blasted the "worst 80th Congress" and denounced the Republicans as the defender of "the privileged few", while he and the Democratic Party – "the people's party" – fought for "the common everyday man". He condemned the Congress for inaction on housing, health care, labour relations, education, the minimum wage, and civil rights. Truman then stunned the hall by announcing that he was calling the Congress back into a special session on 26 July, and demanded that they take up his legislative agenda.

---

* Hamby, 448.

On July 26, Truman gave a speech to Congress restating his demand that it pass his legislative package. As Truman had expected, and probably hoped, it passed no laws over the ensuing fortnight, which gave him the opportunity to hit the campaign trail again denouncing the "do-nothing" Republican Congress. He contrasted congressional inaction with his own activism, issuing Executive Order 9981 on the same day Congress reconvened, which desegregated the US Armed Forces (previously African-Americans and other minorities were put in separate units and treated differently).

Truman was still an underdog in the 1948 election. The Democratic Party had split into three as the election approached. Truman faced not only a challenge to his right in the form of Strom Thurmond and the Dixiecrats, but to his left as well. Henry Wallace had established his own Progressive Party, taking many Democratic-supporting liberals with him. Wallace criticised Truman's hard-line approach to the Soviet Union, denouncing his foreign policy as a threat to world peace. The Republicans had nominated the popular New York governor, Thomas Dewey, as their presidential candidate. Truman was now one candidate in a four-way race for the presidency and most commentators confidently expected that, with the once unstoppable Democratic coalition fractured, Truman would be defeated.

Dewey consistently led in most polls in advance of the election, sometimes by double-digit margins. But he was seen as stiff and uncharismatic compared with the energetic Truman. While Dewey campaigned like a front-runner – aloof and rarely attacking the administration too aggressively – Truman was fighting for his political life. On the night of the election, the *Chicago Daily Tribune* was so confident that Truman had lost that it pre-emptively went to press with the headline: "Dewey Defeats Truman". It was therefore something of a shock to all observers when Truman actually won the election, beating Dewey by almost two million votes. A photograph of a beaming Truman holding the *Tribune*'s front page aloft at a public appearance after his re-election has become the best-known image of the campaign.

The Fair Deal

In his domestic agenda, Truman sought to build on Roosevelt's legacy, accomplishing those reforms that FDR had left unfinished, including a full employment act and national health insurance. That agenda had mostly stalled during his first years in office, particularly after the Republicans won control of Congress in 1946. With his own mandate after the 1948 election, and with the Democrats having won back the House of Representatives and the Senate, Truman renewed his push for reform.

President Truman, soon after being elected as President, proudly holds a copy of the Chicago Tribune *which wrongly predicted his electoral defeat on its front page.*

In his State of the Union message in January 1949, Truman declared that "every segment of our population and every individual has a right to expect from our Government a fair deal".* His domestic agenda came to be known as the "Fair Deal", a phrase that both tied it to and distinguished it from Roosevelt's New Deal. The Fair Deal was as ambitious as any programme FDR had put forward: national health insurance, an expansion of Social Security, a minimum wage raise, repeal of the Taft-

---

* Hamby, 488.

Hartley labour law, federal aid to education, public housing, and civil rights for African-Americans.

Even with his election victory, and Democratic congressional majorities, Truman struggled to pass the Fair Deal. Most of the legislation was blocked by an alliance of Southern Democrats and conservative Republicans. But, as Alonzo Hamby notes, polling reveals that there was limited public support for the "major new federal initiatives" that made up the Fair Deal. Those liberals who expected "a legislative blitzkrieg and a sweep to total victory" were disappointed. Many blamed Truman for a lack of leadership.*

He was, nonetheless, able to amass a solid record of accomplishment in his domestic policy. On the issue of African-American civil rights, this was to have profound implications not only for the nation, but for the structure of the Democratic Party itself. Truman had been committed to some civil rights for African-Americans since first assuming office (though it would be going too far to call him a believer in complete racial equality). In December 1946, he set up a President's Committee on Civil Rights to suggest ways of strengthening civil rights protections. The Committee published its report, "To Secure These Rights", in October 1947, calling for a federal anti-lynching law and the abolition of restrictions that prevented African-Americans from voting, such as poll taxes. It also called for an

---

* Hamby, 493-94.

end to segregation on interstate public transport and in the US army. Such measures failed in Congress, but Truman was able to push them forward with executive orders, such as the aforementioned Executive Order 9981. In 1948, Truman became the first Democratic president to be elected on a party platform (i.e. manifesto) that called explicitly for civil rights reforms.

The decision to commit himself so unequivocally to the cause of civil rights would transform the Democratic Party over the next decades. The election-winning Democratic coalition that Franklin Roosevelt had pulled together rested on an uneasy alliance between Northern liberals and Southern conservatives. Both factions were united in their support for New Deal measures to combat the Depression, but harmony invariably broke down on issues of civil rights. Though Roosevelt won much African-American support because of his anti-recession programmes, beginning a relationship between black Americans and the Democratic Party that continues to this day, he did little to combat the scourge of racism and racial discrimination, for fear of upsetting the Southern elements in the New Deal coalition.

But African-American activism had been building throughout the Second World War. Particularly in the South, black Americans faced segregation in shops, restaurants, public transport, and all kinds of public buildings, and were largely denied the right to vote through such measures as literacy tests and poll taxes. At the outbreak of the war, African-Americans enrolled in the US armed forces in disproportionately high numbers, though usually in segregated units, and many hoped that this service would give them leverage to demand civil and political rights after the war ended. Black activist groups continued the pressure for reform.

In 1941, faced with a possible protest march on Washington, President Roosevelt agreed to issue an executive order prohibiting racial discrimination in the defence industries. Many Southern African-Americans had moved to Northern and Western states, where there were fewer barriers to voting, to work in those defence industries, which strengthened black voters as a political force. Moreover, the race hatred of the fascist regimes that the US was fighting in the war, and post-war revelations about the Holocaust, made American racism less defensible. These considerations were on Truman's mind when formulating his civil rights policies and together they explain why he chose to be more forceful in pursuing them than FDR. But progress was slow. Despite the incremental gains of the 1940s, it would be more than a decade before the passage of the Civil Rights Act (1964) and the Voting Rights Act (1965).

Korea and McCarthy, 1949-1953

Truman's second term was dominated by two things: the "Second Red Scare", embodied in the anti-Communist crusade of Senator Joe McCarthy, and the Korean War.* It was Truman's handling of both that led to him leaving office in 1953 with the lowest approval ratings of any US president. The beginning of the Cold War, and the widespread sense of a Soviet threat to the US, led to a surge of anti-Communist sentiment in domestic politics that verged at times on hysteria. The American public was particularly concerned about Communist espionage in the US and the possibility of Communist infiltration of the government. In Congress, the House Un-American Activities Committee (HUAC), which had been created in 1938, investigated Communist subversion and Americans with suspected Communist sympathies. HUAC's hearings extended into almost all areas of American life. In 1947, investigating whether Communist spies or sympathisers had been planting propaganda in American films, HUAC cited ten screenwriters and directors who refused to testify at their hearings for contempt of Congress. The "Hollywood Ten" were "blacklisted", i.e.

* The "First Red Scare" (1919-1920) had followed World War One, and had been marked by widespread labour unrest and government suppression of radical activists and agitators.

denied any further work in the film industry. The "blacklist" lasted until 1960.

The most famous HUAC investigation was that of Alger Hiss, a State Department official who was accused of having been a Communist spy by Whittaker Chambers, a former Communist himself, in testimony to the committee. Hiss denied the allegations under oath and sued Chambers for defamation. When Chambers produced fresh evidence proving that Hiss had been a Communist agent in the 1930s, Hiss was convicted of perjury and imprisoned. (He was not tried for espionage because the statute of limitations had passed.) Truman mishandled the scandal by dismissing the allegations against Hiss as a "red herring". Hiss had been involved in the setting up of the UN and also in the negotiations at Yalta (the wartime summit which settled the division of Europe into areas of Western and Soviet influence) which fuelled Republican accusations that Eastern Europe was under Soviet control because of the co-operation of treacherous American officials.

Ambitious politicians made use of red-baiting tactics (accusing their opponents of being soft on Communism or even having Communist sympathies) to advance their careers. One of the most skilful was Richard Nixon, a congressman from California who would later become president. In his 1950 campaign for the Senate, Nixon denounced his Democratic opponent, Helen Gahagan Douglas, as "the Pink Lady" who was "pink right down to her underwear". Nixon won the election with 59 per cent of the vote and Douglas never ran for political office again. Truman was contemptuous of Nixon, whom he said was one of only two people in politics he genuinely hated.*

The most notorious red-baiter in these years was a man who has lent his name to both the era and a style of politics ("McCarthyism"). In 1950, Senator Joseph McCarthy, a hitherto undistinguished senator from Wisconsin, gave a speech at the Republican Women's Club in Wheeling, West Virginia, during which he claimed to have a list of 205 Communists working in the State Department. After the speech, McCarthy telegraphed the White House claiming to have a list of 57 names, and a week after that, in a speech to the Senate, he claimed he had a list of 81 names. The number changed all the time and he dodged when asked for specifics.

Though McCarthy engaged in a campaign of smear and innuendo, he proved a remarkably adept exploiter of the press and built a popular following as a no-nonsense opponent of Communist subversion. Truman condemned him privately but refused to confront him publicly. Historians have been divided since then over whether Truman could have stopped McCarthy by issuing a forceful public condemnation. The senator would remain a prominent public figure until 1954 when his

* Dallek, 88.

popularity collapsed after he chaired a controversial series of hearings relating to the US Army.

Though Truman was disgusted by red-baiting demagogues such as McCarthy, he was by no means immune to public demands for anti-Communist measures. In 1947, for instance, he set up a Loyalty Program, requiring all federal government employees to take a loyalty oath and be subject to background checks to determine whether they had ever been involved with "totalitarian, fascist, communist, or subversive" organisations.

International pressures were a spur to anti-Communist efforts at home. By 1949, it seemed to many Americans that they were losing the Cold War. That year, the Soviets successfully tested an atomic bomb and the US lost the nuclear monopoly that it had enjoyed since the end of World War Two. In 1950, a month after Alger Hiss's conviction for spying, British authorities arrested Klaus Fuchs, a scientist who had worked on the Manhattan Project, for passing information about the nuclear weapons programme to Soviet agents. This only stoked American fears about the extent of Communist infiltration of their government. Truman responded by authorising the construction of a hydrogen bomb, a "super bomb" that would enable the US to regain the advantage in nuclear weapons. Also in 1949, the Chinese Civil War, which had been intermittently unfolding since 1927, climaxed with a Communist takeover by forces led by Mao Zedong. Many Republicans blamed the Truman administration for "losing" China to Communism.

Truman's response to these developments was to commission the State Department to prepare a top-secret report into US policy towards the Soviet Union. That report, NSC-68 ("United States Objectives and Programs for National Security") outlined a strategy that called for the quadrupling of the American defence budget, increased aid to US allies, and US commitment to the policy of "containment". Truman was sceptical of the report at first, wary of such massive increases in defence expenditure, though he did not reject it. However, debates over the wisdom of NSC-68 were overtaken by North Korea's invasion of South Korea in 1950.

A former Japanese possession, Korea had been occupied by Allied forces after World War Two: the North by the Soviets, the South by the US. Plans for the reunification of the country ultimately failed, and in 1948 the nation was formally divided into two new republics at the 38th parallel: North Korea and South Korea. North Korea became a Communist state with Kim Il-Sung as premier. South Korea became a capitalist democracy and US ally. In June 1950, with Stalin's backing, North Korean forces invaded the South, with the intention of reunifying Korea, by force, under Communist leadership. The "loss" of China the year before had badly damaged the Truman administration's prestige, and the president was determined not to let another Asian country fall to Communism. "Korea is the Greece of the Far East," Truman told one aide.*

At US instigation, the UN condemned the attack (the Soviet Union, then boycotting the UN, was not able to veto the resolution). North Korea moved quickly, though, capturing South Korea's capital, Seoul, and almost ending the war in days. The commander of US forces in Asia, Douglas MacArthur, appealed to Truman to be allowed to redeploy American forces stationed in Japan to South Korea. Truman agreed and, under MacArthur's command, US forces were able to put down the North Korean advance. By September, Seoul had been retaken and by October, North Korean forces had been driven out of South Korea.

Truman now had to decide whether to stop at the 38th parallel and pursue a peace treaty, or (as MacArthur wanted) to push on into North Korea and try to liberate that nation from Communist rule. Concerned that a US invasion might prompt intervention from China or the Soviet Union, Truman ordered MacArthur to proceed cautiously: to cross the 38th parallel, but to keep US units away from the areas bordering the USSR or China. MacArthur largely ignored those orders, however, and by November Chinese divisions had entered the conflict.

---

* Dallek, 106.

At a face-to-face meeting on Wake Island in October 1950, MacArthur had assured Truman that the fighting would be over by Thanksgiving. It was now clear that the Korean War was becoming much wider and more protracted than Truman wanted. In early 1951, the president offered negotiations to North Korea and China to restore the border at the 38th parallel, and the pre-war status quo. By this point, MacArthur's public pronouncements were becoming increasingly irritating to the White House and, in April, Truman relieved him of his command. However, MacArthur was a national hero and Truman's decision proved enormously controversial. Republican Senator Robert Taft called for Truman's impeachment and MacArthur received a parade when he arrived back in the US.

Peace talks began in July 1951, but they would continue for almost two years – as would the fighting. By the time an armistice was concluded in 1953, Truman had left office and his successor, Dwight D. Eisenhower, received the credit for having successfully ended the war. The combination of the stalemate in Korea, the controversial decision to dismiss MacArthur, and a succession of Communist spy scandals meant that by February 1952, Truman recorded the lowest job approval ratings of any president in modern history (22 per cent). They were still hovering in the 20s by the time he left office a year later.

Harry Truman and the historians

Truman's post-presidential years were difficult. He returned to Independence with his family, where he would live for the rest of his life. In the first years he faced consistent financial hardship. There was no financial support for former presidents or senators, and Truman's only steady source of income was his meagre army pension. It was not until the Former Presidents' Act of 1958 that he began to receive an annual pension. Prior to that, he set a new precedent by becoming the first former president to secure a lucrative book deal for his memoirs.

He re-emerged intermittently to pass comment on important issues. He remained a partisan Democrat, periodically denouncing his Republican successor Dwight Eisenhower for supposedly trying to turn the clock back on the New Deal. He opposed John F. Kennedy's candidacy in 1960, believing Kennedy was both too young and too likely to rely on his father, Joseph Kennedy, whom Truman distrusted for his opposition to FDR and pro-appeasement stance in the 1930s. "It's not the Pope that worries me," he was quoted as saying, in a reference to the controversy about Kennedy's Catholic faith, "it's the pop." In 1965, he attended the ceremony (deliberately held in Independence) at which President Lyndon Johnson signed the law establishing Medicare, a national health insurance programme for older Americans – one of the key components of the Fair Deal that he had been unable to pass almost 20 years earlier.

Truman died in December 1972 and, although his popular reputation had been steadily recovering since he left office, posthumously he enjoyed a remarkable, if brief, burst of popularity. In the mid-1970s, according to one newspaper, "Truman-mania" swept America. In 1974, Merle Miller published *Plain Speaking*, a collection of interviews between the author and Truman conducted some 12 years earlier – the book stayed on the *New York Times*'s bestseller list for over a year. `in 1975, the progressive rock band Chicago released "Harry Truman", which began: "American needs you/ Harry Truman". Playwright Samuel Gullu penned "Give 'Em Hell, Harry!", a one-man play set during the 1948 presidential campaign and starring James Whitmore as Truman. Gerald Ford attended the premiere in Washington, DC, and the play was recorded for a theatrical release, with Whitmore receiving an Academy Award nomination for Best Actor. Truman's new popularity was connected to the political crisis that resulted from Watergate, the criminal conspiracy that forced President Richard Nixon to resign. The blunt and plain-spoken Truman was exactly the sort of leader that a scandal-hit nation was looking for.

After initial negative judgement, a scholarly turnaround in Truman's reputation began with the publication of two biographies in the 1990s: David McCullough's *Truman* (1992) and Alonzo L. Hamby's *Man of the People* (1995), which won the Pulitzer Prize. Of the two, McCullough was the more admiring. Truman was, he wrote, "the kind of president the founding fathers had in mind for the country. He came directly from the people."* Hamby was more cautious: he said that he sought to "demythologize" Truman, but not "debunk him". Truman was, he wrote nonetheless, "one of the most important presidents of our era".**

Initial interpretations of the Truman administration had concentrated on Truman's failures: his belligerence towards the Soviet Union, the scandals that beset his administration, and foreign policy quagmires such as the Korean War. McCullough and Hamby's works triggered a series of new and more sympathetic reappraisals of Truman's time in office. A president who was widely reviled when he retired now routinely makes it into the top ten when historians are asked to rank presidents – in the "great" or "near great" category.

Many of Truman's political and policy decisions will remain controversial. Historians will go on contesting his decision to drop the atomic bomb on Japan, for example, or his handling of domestic anti-communism. However, as the first president to confront the challenges of the Cold War, whose decisions shaped the way all subsequent presidents

---

* McCullough, 991.
** Hamby, viii.

handled that conflict, he is undeniably one of the most consequential holders of that office in the 20th century.

CHRONOLOGY

1884 Harry S. Truman is born in Lamar, Missouri.

1890 The Truman family relocates to Independence, Missouri.

1906 Truman takes over the family farm.

1917 Truman sees action in France as the captain of an artillery unit.

1919 Captain Truman returns to the U.S., marries Bess Wallace.

1922 Truman & Jacobson, the haberdashery Truman had opened with a friend, is forced to close amidst recession; Truman wins election as Jackson County's eastern district judge.

1934 Truman is elected to the U.S. Senate.

1940 Truman wins re-election.

1941 The Truman Committee is established. Its investigations bring Truman national fame.

1944 Truman becomes Franklin D. Roosevelt's running mate and then vice president.

1945 Following the death of FDR, Truman becomes president; Truman orders the use of atomic bombs against Japan, ending the Second World War.

1946 Winston Churchill delivers the Iron Curtain speech; George Kennan sends the Long Telegram; the Republicans win back control of Congress.

1947 Truman announces the "Truman Doctrine" and Congress votes an aid package to Greece and Turkey; the President's Committee on Civil Rights publishes its report, "To Secure These Rights".

1948 Congress passes the Marshall Plan for reconstructing Western Europe; Truman issues the executive order to desegregate the armed forces; Truman wins the presidential election in a stunning upset.

1949 The Soviet Union successfully tests an atomic bomb; the "loss" of China.

1950 Alger Hiss is convicted of perjury; Senator Joe McCarthy begins his anti-communist crusade; NSC-68 is produced at Truman's request; the start of the Korean War.

1951 The Korean War stalemates and Truman seeks peace negotiations; General Douglas MacArthur is relieved of his command.

1952 Dwight D. Eisenhower wins the presidency, the first Republican to do so since Herbert Hoover in 1929.

1953 Truman leaves office.

1972 Truman dies.

BIBLIOGRAPHY

Robert Dallek, *Harry S. Truman* (2008).
Part of 'The American Presidents' series by Times Books. A fine, slim book from one of the foremost presidential biographers.

Aida D. Donald, *Citizen Soldier: A Life of Harry S. Truman* (2012).
Like Dallek's, this is another fine, short biography of Truman, well-written, sympathetic and full of lively detail.

John Lewis Gaddis, *The Cold War* (2005).
Gaddis is the most respected of Cold War historians and this book synthesises a long career of research and thought. The first two chapters cover the Truman years, situating it in the broader international context.

Alonzo L. Hamby, *Man of the People: A Life of Harry S. Truman* (1995).
Probably the best single-volume biography of Truman. Scholarly, judicious, and deeply-researched.

David G. McCullough, *Truman* (1992).
Another good single-volume biography of Truman, though

McCullough is aimed more at the general reader. At around 1,000 pages, it's both hugely detailed and not for the faint-hearted!

Merle Miller, *Plain Speaking: An Oral Biography of Harry S. Truman* (1974).
A biography that relies heavily on Truman's own words which, given Truman's blunt style, makes it highly entertaining to read.

CONNELL GUIDES

MORE IN OUR NEW HISTORY SERIES

Guides
The French Revolution
Winston Churchill
World War One
The Rise and Fall of the Third Reich
The American Civil War
Stalin
Lenin
Nelson
The Tudors
Napoleon

The Cold War
The American Civil Rights Movement
The Normans
Russia and its Rulers

Short Guides
Britain after World War Two
Edward VI
Mary I
The General Strike
The Suffragettes

"Connell Guides should be required reading in every school in the country."
Julian Fellowes, creator of *Downton Abbey*

"What Connell Guides do is bring immediacy and clarity: brevity with depth. They unlock the complex and offer students an entry route."
Colin Hall, Head of Holland Park School

"These guides are a godsend. I'm so glad I found them."
Jessica Enthoven, A Level student, St Mary's Calne

"Completely brilliant. I wish I were young again with these by my side. It's like being in a room with marvellous tutors. You can't really afford to be without them, and they are a joy to read."
Joanna Lumley

To buy any of these guides, or for more information, go to
www.connellguides.com
Or contact us on (020)79932644 / info@connellguides.com

LITERATURE GUIDES

Novels and poetry
Emma
Far From the Madding Crowd
Frankenstein
Great Expectations
Hard Times
Heart of Darkness
Jane Eyre
Lord of the Flies
Mansfield Park
Middlemarch
Mrs Dalloway
Paradise Lost
Persuasion
Pride and Prejudice
Tess of the D'Urbervilles
The Canterbury Tales
The Great Gatsby
The Poetry of Robert Browning
The Waste Land
To Kill A Mockingbird
Wuthering Heights

Shakespeare
A Midsummer Night's Dream
Antony and Cleopatra
Hamlet
Julius Caesar
King Lear
Macbeth
Othello
Romeo and Juliet
The Second Tetralogy
The Tempest
Twelfth Night

Modern texts
A Doll's House
A Room with a View
A Streetcar Named Desire
An Inspector Calls
Animal Farm
Atonement
Beloved
Birdsong
Hullabaloo
Never Let Me Go
Of Mice and Men
Rebecca
Spies
The Bloody Chamber
The Catcher in the Rye
The History Boys
The Road
Vernon God Little
Waiting for Godot

NEW
A Short History of English Literature
American literature
Dystopian literature
How to read a poem
How to read Shakespeare
The Gothic
The poetry of Christina Rossetti
Women in literature

First published in 2017 by
Connell Guides
Spye Arch House
Spye Park
Lacock
Wilts
SN15 2PR

10 9 8 7 6 5 4 3 2 1

Copyright © Connell Guides Publishing Ltd.
All rights reserved. No part of this publication
may be reproduced, stored in a retrieval system or transmitted in any
form, or by any means (electronic, mechanical, or otherwise) without
the prior written permission of both the copyright owners
and the publisher.

A CIP catalogue record for this book is available from the British Library.
ISBN 978-1-911187-67-7

Design © Nathan Burton
Assistant Editor and typeset by:
Brian Scrivener and Paul Woodward

Printed in Great Britain

www.connellguides.com